The Real Life Brady Bunch

Kiyua

authorHOUSE®

AuthorHouse™
1663 Liberty Drive, Suite 200
Bloomington, IN 47403
www.authorhouse.com
Phone: 1-800-839-8640

First published by AuthorHouse 12/3/2008

ISBN: 978-1-4389-0620-1 (sc)

Library of Congress Control Number: 2008909525

Printed in the United States of America
Bloomington, Indiana

This book is printed on acid-free paper.

The Real-Life Brady Bunch

This is a story about a family named Brady, the real Brady Bunch. Our story begins with a man named Sherman Brady, from the big D.C., a little town with big initials. Sherman had a brother named Francis Brady, and the two brothers got together with two sisters, named Elsie and Cornelia. The couples starting dating, and soon and very soon they decided to get hitched—both couples, Elsie and Sherman and Francis and Cornelia. From the family of Sherman and Elsie came Sherman Jr., Donald, Maxine, Douglas, Patricia, Gaylord, Michael, Rachell, and William, a family of nine. His brother Francis and Cornelia had Francis Jr., Gerald, Gwen, Reginal, and Craig, a family of five; our first cousins. We all love each other like brothers and sisters and would do anything for one another. Our grandparents on our mother's side were Indians called Blackfoot. Our grandfather's name was Jess and our grandmother's name was Edna; she was sooooooo beautiful, with skin of ivory and hair black and shiny, like silk. My job in the evening was to brush Grandmom's hair for at least one hundred strokes in the same spot. I guess that was a ritual that their culture had to make their hair grow. That's what Grandmom taught us to do.

I would brush all over her head until I had done my hundred strokes all around her head, and then I would finish up with one big braid that hung down the middle of her back. Then she would roll her braid up into one big ball and put a hairpin in it to keep her braid up, and then she would put on her hair cap before bed. Our granddad was a strong man, big and tall, with a heavy voice that scared us when he talked. All he had to do was talk, and you listened. As time passed by, our grandparents passed away. Our grandparents were the greatest grandparents I have ever known. Well, I guess we all say that about our grandparents because we all feel that way about them. Our family lived in the family house for awhile, and then Dad bought a double house right at the corner of Hamilton Street, right at the corner where our family house is. It was two houses joined together, so our brother Donnie and his family lived there, and our uncle and his wife took over the family home along with Uncle Woodley. He was called Woodley because he had a wooden leg and got around using a cane. Uncle Woodley was always at our home. When Mom and Dad needed someone to keep us, it was him. He was a great and fun uncle. He would dance for us with his cane and make sure we were ready for school.

All of us went to an all-black school back then. The school we went to was way back in the boonies, and it was labeled school number 118C. I guess the "C" stood for colored. Well, we didn't notice or care that it was all black students; we knew that it was kind of strange, but we didn't question it. We enjoyed each other and were all good friends. We all walked to and from school. Our school was just past our cemetery, and at first it was kind of scary to have to walk past it. But our mother told us not to be afraid of the people in the cemetery; she said they won't hurt you. But she also said that the ones who will are the ones walking alongside you. They are the people you need to watch out for. And that was and is soooo true. Our school consisted of two classrooms, and we had two teachers. For the first, second, and third grades we had Mrs. Burns, and for the fourth, fifth, and the sixth grades we had Mr. Rollins; they were great teachers, thank God. Mr. Rollins was a teacher who taught us very well. He also taught us discipline; he had a black leather strop, the kind that was used for sharpening razors for shaving. He named it his "Black Gentleman." It was used to correct any problem we had. If we were being rude or bad, he would use it on the one who was being rude or bad. He would take the student into our club room for discipline—it was our restroom and where we hung our coats. There he would take his Black Gentleman, and we all would listen for the cry that never came. Mr. Rollins only wanted to scare you and not to hurt or harm you, even though he had our parents' permission. It was mainly for control in and out of his classroom and to be the boss, and he was. Mr. Rollins had a wooden arm, and he would show us how he would click it up or he would click it down to his side.

We had a dentist come to our school for dental work if needed. A lot of us kids needed some dental work done. I wouldn't let the dentist do my mouth, so Mom had to send my brother to school with me to get his done so I would get mine done too, which I needed. Sherman Jr. was the only person besides Mom and Dad you listened to, and I did. When school was over at the end of the day, we all did our homework and ate supper before we went to play. Then we would meet. If we didn't have softball practice then we would sometimes roller skate or play baseball. If we were going to go skating we would plan it before we all met. Three of us had a job after school twice a week for our teacher Mr. Rollins. We had to cut his grass. The three of us would split the sections into three so we all had our own section to do. After we were done, Mr. Rollins or his wife would fix us a sandwich and give us a cold drink, and then he would pay us for our job.

When we got paid, we headed right downtown to the store to get whatever. I would always go to Mrs. Arkie's to get one of her famous hamburgers. Those burgers were sooo good that it would make you hurt yourself. We—that means all of us—were on a softball team that was coached by everybody's Uncle Bulbie, and it was an awesome team. Our sister Max was the pitcher, and I played shortstop. We won all but two games out of twenty. Our team was called the Mighty Vipers. We had practice every other day after school. That came first, and everything else we wanted to do came after that. We would practice at the D.C. Middle School. They would say practice makes perfect. And we did just that. Back at home our dad would treat us to a day of crabbing on Saturdays. Dad would tell all of us the day before, which was on Friday, that if we wanted to go crabbing with him in the morning, we'd better be up and getting ready to go. That night before, our mom would pack lunch for all of us, and we were good to go. Most of the days we would be there until just after noon. We didn't eat our lunch at lunchtime. We ate it for brunch between breakfast and before lunch. When we were done crabbing, we took our catch home to our mom, and we would spray them off with the hose and then help Mom separate the dead ones from the live ones, if there were any. We had big crab pots that Mom would cook them in. She would season them, and she used a can or two of beer; we wondered what the beer was for, and Mom told us taste, and we thought we would get drunk eating them with the beer in there. While the crabs were cooking, we played until they were done, and we also helped Dad get the picnic table ready. We always had the picnic table under the big tree on the side of our brother Donnie's house. When the crabs were done we all ate, and Dad would have some clams with his friends. We watched them eat them. They would open the clam shell with a knife and would suck them right out of the shell. Uhooo, they seemed to us to be nasty. I still don't mess with them. I guess seeing that turned me off. Well, don't leave out the beer. Dad's mother's house was next to Donnie's; her name was Rachael, so that was Grandmom Rachael. She would spoil us with her homemade popsicles, which were out of this world, and she took care of some people; I can remember some men who were always at her house, eating. There was a man named Em, and they were always under the influence it seemed, and our grandmother was always feeding them. She was always cooking, and she also would sell dinners: all kinds of chicken, fish, chitterlings, and pigs' feet, and they were dinners with sides, and she would also have corn bread. That was a cooking lady. But I can remember how good those popsicles were; they were vanilla, and they were very, very good. Well, back to the crabs: Mom had us shell the crabs that we didn't eat, and she would fry them. She made a batter with bread crumbs, and then she would fry them, um um good. Well, back to after school. Some of the time we all would go swimming. We had two beaches; one was a sandy beach, and that was the beach we used most of the time. Because the other beach was used by big ships after a while, and they would bring in different things like oil and probably animals like water moccasins, we stayed away from that beach, and soon we stayed away from the sandy beach too. The people had built a station for the boats that came in to dock. The big freight boats carried a lot of people—we called them boat people—and when the boats came, our town was overrun by the people. The city bar at the end of town would be running over with people; it was a good thing for our little town, because they would do big business since the people were not afraid to spend their money. But it was really good.

We had two grocery stores, one dry cleaners, one post office, and two gas stations; the dry cleaners was black-owned. Mrs. Mainworm's store was an everything store where she sold everything from clothes to ice cream sandwiches. She made the ice cream sandwiches from half-pint ice cream; they were blocks set between two wafer cones and were sooooo great—and she also owned about ten cats that were all over the place. She would cut and made your ice cream sandwich and leave the knife on the countertop, and those cats would be all over it. And the next person who got an ice cream sandwich would get it without her washing the knife off. How gross. But we knew that and continued to buy her ice cream sandwiches, dirty and all. Then there was Mrs. Morre, who owned the store next door. She sold books, candy, sandwiches, and ice cream. Mother used to do her laundry and some of her housework. I helped her with the house cleaning but not the clothes. Mom would just starch and iron them. I would always take the clothes back when Mom was done. She had mainly shirts, sheets, pillow cases, and boxers—now that took the cake. I had to talk to Mom about that. I asked her why she was ironing her husband's boxer drawers: "Now you don't iron Dad's, and you're not going to iron theirs. If she still wants you to do the rest of her laundry, then it will be fine. If not, that's fine too; but you are not going to iron his drawers. If she wants or needs them ironed, then she should do it, because we don't do boxers like we don't do windows. You are on your own with them both." Her home was on top of the store, and I did the floors and dusting while Mom just had the clothes. And Mrs. Morre also sold fountain sodas. And then there was Mrs. Lucky's; she had to make a lot of money off of me just for her hamburgers. I loved her burgers, and anytime I got enough money to get one, I headed right for her store. I was like Wimpy, only I paid for mine right then and there. I didn't wait for Tuesday. No charge account. They were soooooooo good, I thought I would overdose on them. And there was Mr. Curk; he sold all men's work shoes and work clothes. And a little bit of everything. Then there was a bar and another grocery store, owned by Mr. Corncob, and then there was the dry cleaners, called Mr. Kerry's, and after that there was the post office; on the bottom floor and the top were apartments where our friends lived. Then, going farther down the street, there were about four or five homes, and at the end of that block was the other bar and restaurant. The bar sat across from the city park, and across from the park was a tour boat that took people across the river to Pea Patch Island, where there was a history of war and soldiers. It was a great little historic town where we kids could run loose, and we all knew each other. Our parents also told us all not to play around the canal, which we did not do. We all knew the rules and knew that we were not to talk to strangers. We were surrounded by water, so it really was easy for us to play around it. But there was a time when our brother Doug and his friends thought it would be funny to throw me into the canal, and I didn't know how to swim. They counted to three, and at the count of three said, "Let's get her!" So they counted to three with me fighting to stay above water, and they thought it was funny. When they got me out, I ran home and told Mom just what they did, and my brother got punished big time. Thank God I didn't drown, and my bother never played that game again. We soon learned how to swim back at our school; our school would have what we called play day. That was when we all would compete against each other in games for prizes. And our parents would do all the cooking and barbeque all the meats. We would have such a great time. Mrs. Burns' classes and Mr. Rollins' classes would compete by age groups, and that would go on all day; we enjoyed it, and our teachers would give all the winners gifts and treats. Then we all would get our food and sit to eat and enjoy it. That was really marvelous to see all our parents and teachers and friends together—unforgettable. That left us with a lot of memories that we took with us.

The year our school was to close, we were both sad and glad to become a part of the public school. The schools were to integrate, and we were to integrate with other students. Well, we didn't know what the move meant to us coming from an all-black school and getting ready to enter into a mixed school. The whole picture really didn't matter to us; we welcomed it and most of the time wondered why we were separated from the whites anyway. But there must have been a reason, so no questions were asked, because we were not there for show; we were there to learn, and nothing else should have mattered. Our school was D.C. Middle School, which was nice, as expected, and we did many things together in the sixth, seventh, and eighth grades. By living there in the town we knew just about all the students, because we played together sometimes. And now we were in school together. My sister Max and I learned how to play field hockey. We both liked it and traveled to other schools to play other teams. Now that was fun, hitting that hard ball from one end of the field to the other end; the only problem was that it was too much running, and we tired out fast. We also learned how to play croquet— now that was better. I really enjoyed knocking another wooden ball around. During school after the change, each class voted to have a talent show, and that was right up our alley, because we all thought we were good singers, and I do mean good. Well, my group consisted of Good, Better, and Best. We decided to try to sing the song "In the Still of the Night," and we competed against my brother Doug and his group. We did a lot of practicing and started sounding good, I mean real good. We knew we could win. The night of the talent show we had some real good talent that entered. Our brother and his group were just a little bit better than we were. But we all had a great time and enjoyed it. We all gave them credit where credit was due. As for our parents, it was enormous. They were sooo proud of all of us for doing such a great job. On the way to and from that school there was a strawberry garden where a man and his mother lived. And it was sooo tempting for all of us kids, being right there at the edge of the road; all you had to do was dive in, which we did—many times. And the little lady would come running to chase us away. It seemed that anytime we were trying to get some strawberries, she would catch us. We would dive into the strawberries on our stomachs as if we were swimming, and it was as though she was sitting and waiting for us to make our move. She was always right there to chase us. Right down on the next corner was a man named Hammie Younger who owned a sickle pear tree, and we were always getting some pears. Well, he didn't like that, and he would chase us away from his house. The boys would climb the tree, but the girls would get them from off the ground. We had no business invading their property, but we did. We were not bad kids, but we were mischievous kids, and we were always trying to get something for nothing. We seemed to like teasing older people by taking their strawberries and the sickle pears. As I look back that really wasn't funny or nice—it was being cruel—and I regret that I ever took part in that, but when one does it, the rest follow; that was peer pressure. Talking about strawberries, our mother could make a mean strawberry shortcake. She would send us kids around to Mr. Caul's to pick about three or four pints of strawberries. We walked to Mr. Caul's house, where he had a big strawberry garden, and he would give us the pint baskets for our strawberries. We picked until our baskets were filled, and then we paid him and walked back home with the berries. When we got there with the strawberries, we would wash and stem them while Mom worked on the shortcake; then we sliced the strawberries, put some sugar on top, and mixed them. Then we put them in the refrigerator until the shortcake was done, and ohhh my God. When Mom finished we could hardly contain ourselves; but we didn't get any until after dinner. It was our dessert. And it was um um good.

My oldest sister and my youngest sister always helped Mom with the cooking and cleaning. Mom was everything to us, and to everybody else. She was the town hairdresser, and she would do everyone's hair—that meant all us blacks. And she also did the ears; she pierced everyone's ears and their babies' too. But the babies had to be at a certain age before she would do their ears. Mom was one that they would call jack-of-all-trades and master of none, but here comes that big *but:* She was a jack-of-all-trades and master of all, because you see whatever she set her mind to do, she did it, and she did it very well. Mom could make a mean batch of homemade root beer and homemade doughnuts, and oh yea don't forget those homemade baked beans. And the homemade yeast bread. We enjoyed making the yeast bread because of the steps that Mom took to make it, and just to think that Mom could make bread. She would make the dough, and then we would cover it with a dish towel; that was for the dough to rise. And once the dough had done that, then she would bake it; oh my goodness, that was some dynamite bread. And she would also make it for some people. It took some time to make, but all in all it was great.

Mom would be asked to make for all the barbeques that people were having. Everyone loved her and her cooking. We would start by saving the glass jugs for the root beer. She would always make it around Christmas, and also the doughnuts. We brought cranberry juice in jugs, which we saved to make our root beer in. She started with root beer extract, and from there the root beer was made. Once it was made, she kept it in a warm place and covered it with a sheet or blanket; the reason for that was to help the yeast to work. It would stay that way for about a week, and then we would take the jugs in from the heat and put them in a cool place, the reason being to stop the yeast from working. Now the root beer would stay in a cool place for a couple of days; after that we were able to drink it. And it wasn't long before it was gone. She would make about ten to twelve jugs.

Our mom Elsie and our aunt Cornelia were everybody's aunts, and as it was with their parents we also called them our aunts and uncles. Mom and Aunt Sister were two loving sisters; they were and still are the best that anyone could have asked for. Our mother has passed, but we still have our special aunt, Sister. She is doing well; she has her ups and downs, but don't we all. But all in all we all love her to death. She also has a very very good son. He is also special, and he takes very good care of her. Thank God for him. Good job; you go, Danny! Our hats are off to you for doing such a great job. One day when Mom was living, we decided to go into the family house; well, no one was living there at the time. It was Mom, Shelly, and myself, and we didn't know what was in there. Well, it wasn't much, but we did find Uncle Woodley's cane in a closet. We went upstairs, and on top of the mantel was a clock. I asked Mom about it, and she said it belonged to Mom Edna, but that it stopped working when Mom was living. It didn't work anymore. And, me being me, I was curious, so I picked the clock up, and all of a sudden it started working. Mom looked at me and I looked at her. She then asked me what I did, and I told her I just picked it up. That was kind of scary. But then we knew that Grandmom Edna's spirit was there with us. That was her sign, to let us know that she was glad the clock started working. We didn't take the clock with us; we just left it in its rightful place and left after that. But we did take Uncle Woodley's cane.

Now going back in the day, Dad's aunt and our aunt Isabel had what they called back then a juke joint, which was a bar and a dance place where the blacks could go and enjoy themselves with each other, and they did enjoy it, until one day or night it caught on fire and could not be saved. So the juke joint had to be demolished, and it was. Aunt Isabel had a house built on the property. And that was and is a nice house. My cousin Itsey lived there after that with her family; she had two boys and two girls. When she passed away, our uncle and aunt brought the house, and they now rent it out. Right across from that house was what we used to call the station. Well, I can remember that Dad had a house put on that lot. We lived there for awhile. I never knew why it was called the station, but right down from our house were some tracks, like train tracks, and I remember that people used to go fishing back there. I knew that there were some snakes back there, so I didn't go there. The railroad tracks were over the water, and they would sit on the old tracks to fish.

Back to our home on Hamilton: When school was out for the summer, we always went on summer school trips, and we would always go to Fort Delaware to Pea Patch Island. We didn't have to go out of our town to get history—it was right there. We had fun running in and out of the dungeons and learning about the history of our soldiers, seeing the chains that were hanging in the dungeons, and seeing and learning about the weapons that they used. It was great to know that all this took place right across the river from where we lived. There once was some big excitement, but our best trips were the ones that our church took. And that was to Willow Grove amusement park, where we could run wild and ride on whatever we wanted. Mom would pack a big lunch for us; it would be fried chicken, potato salad, drinks, and snacks. And fruit. We were so excited when we arrived at the park, and we went to get a picnic table and lay out all our food. And we had to eat before we got to go on to the park. We wanted to just go. But we did eat, and we all stuffed our mouths with food just to hurry up; we were impatient and wanted just to go. And when we were finished we all went wild. When the day was ending and it was time to depart, we were sad to have to leave. But we were ready. Mom and Dad enjoyed knowing that we all had such a good time, and we would tell them about what we did and what we all rode on. We all had the best time. When we arrived back home, we got our clothes ready for Sunday school and church.

We sang in the church choir, and we loved and enjoyed it. We sang in the junior choir; there was also a senior choir and the men's choir. Oh my God, they were grrrrreat. We had three uncles who sang in that choir. Our choir traveled to other churches, and other churches traveled to our church; they were some really good days. We all loved it. I can't sing now, but I wish I could do it all over again. Two of our uncles built their own homes, and they were brick homes. The houses had a basement and a fireplace and walk-in showers. These were part of a home that I wasn't used to but just had dreams about. I loved both of them and wished that we lived in a home like that. The homes are beautiful, and our cousin still lives in one; the other one was sold. Both uncles have passed away, but they left their mark, and it was and is such a great accomplishment for both of them. Great job, and kudos. Our oldest sister Maxine, aka Sissy, was asked to attend the prom, and I think we were more excited than she was, because Sissy is a great sister, and she really didn't go anywhere. I was always the wild one, so it was very exciting; for Mom and Dad too. Well, Mom and Sissy went shopping for her dress and shoes. She picked out a blue spaghetti-strap dress; it was nice and had shoes to match, and they were nice too. Well, she went to the prom, and we had to know all about it. So she enjoyed herself and had a good time, for which we all were glad. She was so pretty the night of the prom; she looked like a princess. Soon after, when no one was home but me, I decided to try on her dress and shoes to see what I looked like. Well, the dress was too long on me and the heels were too high. Nothing was right for me. I know I sound like the three bears—nothing was right with them either. So I went to work on the dress, cutting it to my length. And I sawed the heel of the shoes down; once I did, the toe of the shoes stood straight in the air, and I still didn't look right. So, me being me, I had to hide them, because I messed them up. And when Sissy couldn't find them, she asked Mom where they were, and she did not know. I was the next choice. She asked me, and I had to confess what I had done. Not only did I mess up her things, but I messed up her memories. I so regret that, but me being me, as I said, I would do something like that at that time as a kid. Did I get in trouble? Yes, I did. When we talk about what I did back then, we have a good laugh. I can't believe I could have done that, but I did. I had a shoe fetish, and I still do: I love me some shoes, and boots. When our mother got paid from her job, which was every two weeks, she would give her whole paycheck to me and our brother Doggie, and we were to get what we needed, not what we wanted. And Mom would be all right with that. And she never ever complained; she was just happy to see that we were happy. I was one of the singers and the dancer of our family and more or less the clown. I was, and I do mean was, a pretty good singer. Whenever Dad came home feeling pretty good, Mom would tell me that when Dad came home not to play his music. And when he called for me to play his song, I would jump from my bed and get his record, which was Fats Domino, "Blueberry Hill." He wasn't bothering anyone, and it made me happy to see him happy. That was something that he enjoyed—listening to his music and singing. I guess that is where I got it from, because whenever Mom was at her friend's house sometimes she would call me to come and sing for them, like a little monkey that gets paid for dancing. Sometimes I would get money, and the song I remember the most was "Blowing in the Wind" by Stevie Wonder. Oh I danced and sang my heart out for them to make them proud, and I knew that they were, and that is of all their children. But most of the time, when Dad made lunches, he would ask us what kind of cookie we wanted in our lunch, and I loved Vienna Fingers, so that is what I wanted. And Sissy wanted Fig Newtons. Well, every time Dad would come back with Vienna Fingers, and I started feeling bad, because Sissy didn't get what she wanted. So the next time Dad asked us, I said that we wanted Fig Newtons. Well, I didn't like them, but it seemed that Sissy would get what she wanted. It made me sad to think that Dad only got my cookies and not hers. Our little sister Rachell, aka Shelly, always felt as if Dad favored me, and at the time I would think that too. It made me sad to think that Dad would like one child over the other. It also makes me sad for her to say that he was and is my dad and not hers. And I would tell her that he was her dad and all of our dad. Even though he might not show it at times, he loved us all. And I knew that I was the middle girl, meaning that I had a sister older than me and a sister younger. Then we had to do our chores, like cleaning and mainly dishes. We didn't mind cleaning, but when it came to dishes, Sissy and I would take turns. Shelly was not doing dishes at that time, so we were always getting our turns messed up. But it really wasn't messed up; it was just that I was trying to get out of my turn, because I probably didn't want to do them. So Dad fixed that; he had us do dishes for a week at a time. We didn't get messed up again, and that worked for us. Our grandmother Rachael—that's our dad's mom—sold her house to a family that had children who were the same age as our family, so we became friends with them all. The boys became buddies, and the same with us girls, since they had girls our age too. We all became friends, and that was a good thing. The boys were always competing against each other, and one always thought he was better than the others. They all were best on the football field and the basketball court. They all could play ball. They all received trophies and were honored many times. They really carried the team most of the time, if not all of the time. They were popular on and off the team and also were popular with the girls, which swelled up their heads. One of our brothers was not into sports as much as the others; he was more into cars. He liked Chevys and got himself one—a '65 Chevy; that was nice, and he just loved it. Well, he started dating one of Mrs. Harrah's daughters, and they were madly in love. From that marriage came a son, and he was named after his dad. But before that, he decided to go out of town for awhile. Where he went, we didn't know, but he was told that where he was they were now his family; they were his mother, father, sister, and brother. So when he came home he was strange, different, whatever you wanted to call it; but he wasn't him. And he started giving Mom a little bit of a hard time. And Mom being Mom would put up with it because he was still her child. Well, it went on for awhile, and we told Mom that he needed help, so she tried to get him some. But he had to hurt someone or someone had to hurt him before they could help him. Well, he was not what he claimed to be. But he did slice his wrist, and he cut veins and all. He had to have many surgeries, and had stayed in the hospital for a long time, so long that he had to be admitted to a long-term care hospital, where he passed. When he was in the hospital, he needed to have another surgery, but he wouldn't let the doctor operate anymore, and the doctor told us that he needed it. So my sister Shelly went to visit him, and we had a long talk. He was looking pretty good for what he had been through, but we talked about the surgery that he still needed. And he said that he didn't want any more, so I told him that he had to have it done, and I wanted him to have it; well, he said he would. But I don't know if he was just telling me that he would to make us feel better. I remember that when Shelly and I were leaving after visiting hours, I looked back at him through his window, and I saw a tear coming down. That made me feel so bad, but he had to have the surgery. And still today I can see the tear. We miss and love you, Michael. He married the girl next door, as I mentioned before, and from that marriage came a son, his namesake, who looks just like his dad. And now he has two beautiful daughters, Michael's grandaughters, and my friend that lived next door, we were always together. We also had another girlfriend, and we all hung out together. Her boyfriend and my boyfriend were from the same town, and they also hung out together. Well, we were Good, Better, and Best. That is the name that our teacher gave us. Best was the one who got pregnant with child, and it was as if we all were pregnant, because it seemed as if we had her symptoms. We all knew that we were going to help take care of her baby, so in other words we were going to raise the baby with her mother. She was having a baby girl. When the time came, she gave birth to a beautiful and healthy baby girl. Her mother named her after me, so she is my namesake. And we took good care of her, her mother and Good and Better. When she was old enough, she traveled right along with us, and where we went she went. She grew up to be a beautiful young lady and is married to a loving husband. We are so proud of how she turned out. A job well done. Kudos to us. She has all the respect in the world, so you see she never had to ask her mother to keep or babysit her baby, because we were there. And the saying that it takes a village to raise a child is so true. When our boyfriends came to our town, I was having my sixteenth birthday, and we all walked up to our school, which was called the lovers' spot. I didn't know about that; it wasn't that to me. Well, I guess my friend had a different agenda, and he thought that was the reason for us being there. And, me being me, I wasn't that type. Nor was I ready for what he thought I was. Well, I cut that short: Nothing is happening here. Best had her friend drive his car there, and we were in the car, and when I thought he was getting fresh, I jumped out of the car and ran all the way home. And guess what: I didn't look back. When I got home I tried to avoid our front steps that squeaked, but you know how that is: I think I hit everyone of them. And then I knew that Mom or Dad would be standing at the top waiting for me. Well, I guess I felt guilty for nothing, but because I had put myself in that situation I felt like I was guilty. But thank God— Mom and Dad were still asleep. You should have seen how fast I got into my bed. But I learned a lesson; it was that I didn't go that way anymore. The trust left, and I was always on guard. That was too close for comfort. The next day, Best and I laughed about it. She didn't know why I did what I did, and that was to run home. That was a close call. I was such a tomboy that when one time another boy who was my friend thought he could kiss me, I threw him over my back. I thought I would never hear the end of that; they teased and laughed about that for days. Now that was funny. My friends told everyone what I had done and said not to mess with me. While I was dating my friend, he had many other girlfriends. So one day my cousin Franny told me, "Cuz, may the best woman win." Well, I guess I was the best woman, because I won, and now we've been married for forty-one years. From the marriage we have two children; the oldest is Dawn, and our son is Harold, aka Pete. The nickname Pete was after our father. And Dawn has the middle name Unique from our brother Gaylord, aka Skippy. It came about because one night while we were asleep, Skippy was dreaming, and he called out, "You're neat," and I thought he said "unique," so that is how she got her middle name. Our sister Shelly is a great person, and she loves Dawn very much, and she also did and would do anything for her.

So one day Shelly went to get Dawn some ice, and her hands were wet at the time, so her fingers got frozen to the freezer. She could not get loose, nor could she get her ice, so she sent Dawn to Mrs. Harrah's house to get help. Well, when Dawn went to Mrs. Harrah's house, she didn't tell her what was going on, so Mrs. Harrah thought she wanted a treat, so that is what she got. When Dawn went back to Shelly, Shelly was looking for help, and there was Dawn standing there with a treat, so she knew she was still in trouble. She heard the garbage truck, and she knew the crew that worked on the truck. The screen door to the kitchen was open, so she knew that if she hollered loud enough he would hear her. So that is what she did. Reese heard her, but he knew that Shelly was a jokester, so he didn't pay her any attention. He didn't believe her, and he continued working. So there she was, wondering what to do, and she noticed the hot curlers on top of the refrigerator. She really had to reach, and if she missed them, they could go farther back. So she reached for them and got a hold of them, and then she started chipping away until she was free. She still has the freezer burns on those fingers that were stuck. She didn't realize that pouring water on her fingers while they were already stuck to the ice just made the situation worse, but she soon found out. After that, she was so mad at Dawn, and I can relate to that, because there was a time when I was watching Shelly, and somehow she found a penny, and before I could get it, she had it in her mouth and swallowed it, and she was choking. Oh my God! I know there is a God. I had her standing on her head, literally, while I was pounding on her back. All at once the penny came out, and she was scared and crying, and so was I. Thank you Jesus! My heart was in my throat, and so I was choking along with her. That's how scared I was. Whenever my friends and I went anywhere I had to take Shelly with us. She had to tag along behind us. Well, I knew what that was for: so she could tell Mom what I did. I told her she'd better not tell Mom what I do, or she would not get any more candy. I didn't have to worry about her. She wanted that candy, so she kept quiet. My two friends and I were nicknamed "The Three Stooges," "The Three Musketeers," and last but not least, the name that we liked the most: "Good, Better, and Best"—that name came from our teacher, Mr. Rollins. So that was the one we were stuck with. But we didn't mind that one at all. We liked it. I was Good, and

Pudding was Better, and Baby Girl was Best. We are all still close to each other, and we have a great laugh at the things we used to do. But they were all in fun.

Our mother enjoyed going to bingo, and so did I. Her friend Maul would go with Mom when I didn't, but mainly it would be Mom, Maul, sometimes Peggy, Hess, and me. We traveled up and down the road to go to bingo wherever it was. We took turns driving, and we had so much fun even if we didn't win anything. Well, this one night it was just Mom and Maul, and Maul did the driving. We mainly traveled the back roads to avoid the traffic and miss most of the lights. Well, this night, when they were coming home from bingo, Mom said she saw a strange thing at the edge of the road, and she said that it had big feet and it looked like it was shuffling into the bushes, and it was hairy. She said she'd better not say anything to Maul, because she might think Mom was seeing things; so she didn't. But she noticed that Maul had slowed up, so Mom asked her why she did that. And she said, "Essie"—she called Mom Essie, not Elsie—but she said, "Did you see that?"
Mom said, "Yes, but I didn't say anything because I didn't know if you had seen it." And she said, "Yes, I saw it." So she told Maul to get them out of there, and they did, and they didn't look back. Mom said it looked like Bigfoot. So that was proof that they both did see something. And then there was another time, when I didn't go again, but Mom, Maul, and Uncle James went. Uncle James drove. So this time on the way back, Mom and all of them were getting sleepy, but Mom tried to stay awake, because she knew that Uncle James was dozing off. But she dozed off too. And

lo and behold Uncle James lost control of the car, and Mom said that when she and Maul woke up, the car had gone over a hump and they were in the bushes. Well, all was OK, and they were not hurt. But I told Mom that we'd better leave bingo alone. Well, here it comes again, and this time Mom owned a Ford LTD. It was a nice car, and this time I went with them. Maul drove, and it was Mom, Cousin Peggy, and me. Since we didn't take Mom's car, Shelly wanted to use it, so Mom left her car keys with Shelly. Well, Shelly's boyfriend came to get her, so she left with him, and she left the keys. She told Donna and Billy to let Mom know where her keys were when she got back. Well, they got their heads together, and the light bulb went off. Donna was the oldest, so she did the driving and Billy was the passenger. They went driving around and were having fun and thought they were in the clear, but when they drove past Cousin Peggy's house, they saw her car. Not knowing what car we went to bingo in, they just knew we were back from bingo. So Donna got nervous and lost control of the car. Peggy's house was right across from the canal, and that is where she drove the car. Now mind you, Billy could swim, but Donna couldn't, so Billy was scared that she would drown if she could get out. Well, they both got out of the car through the windows, and Billy said that he looked around and saw Donna pass him doing the doggie paddle. So they both got to shore. They knew that they both were in trouble, big trouble, so Donna went into hiding, but Billy didn't; he thought that just because he wasn't driving, he wasn't in trouble. Wrong they both were. When we got back from bingo, we noticed all of the commotion that was going on, and all of the cops at the canal right down from our house. Well, Mom's car wasn't home, so we knew that Shelly had it. When we let Peggy off at home, the cop told us that someone had gone overboard in their car. We were curious and wanted to see it when they pulled the car out. There was a person who'd seen it go over, and just about the spot. But he hadn't seen if the person or people got out, so we all assumed that the person was still in the car. Once they pulled the car out, and we saw that it was Mom's car, we just flipped. Mom found out that it was Donna and Billy, and Donna's dad was fit to be tied, knowing that it was his daughter. He went looking for her with the mind to hurt her once he found her. Mom told him that he was not going to touch her. Well, Mom found out where she was and got her out of hiding, but get this: Mom hid her from her dad. Well, Donna was the boy that Donnie never had. He was blessed with five girls, and he knew he didn't need a boy, because he was enough. Donna is the oldest girl, and she was Mom's pet. Mom loved them all, but her Donna could do no wrong and was her number one even after destroying her car. She could do no wrong in Mom's eye. All she had to say was "Bram"—that is what she called Mom. She also lived with us, and you know the saying "Practice what you preach"? Well, a couple of weeks after Donna's and Billy's incident, her dad Donnie, who was always into something himself—he was a big man—did the same that his daughter did. He was feeling good, as usual, and he drove the car he was driving into the canal too. The car was all electrical, and he said that the windows were halfway down, and he came out of that window. We don't know how, but he did. So you see he was ready to hurt his daughter for the same thing that he did—driving the car overboard. He also went down on a motorcycle, and he only got scrapes and brush burns. And that was without a helmet because he didn't believe in following the rules. He would break them all. Luck was his mark; he was born with a veil over his face—Mom explained to us what that meant, and she said that it means good luck. One time we were all at home, and Grandmom and Mom were at church. Somehow Donnie and I got into an argument, but it was more like a fight, and I knew that it was time to break loose after I threw a fork in his leg and it stuck there. I busted out the front door, and I headed right for the church, where Grandmom and Mom were. He was running on my heels, but I was a good runner. And he was light on his feet—he could run. I got to the church first and was out of breath. I ran up the church steps, and church was in service, but I busted through the door and fell right down in the aisle. Everyone's eyes were on me, of course. Mom and Grandmom got up and took me out of the church to see what was going on. And Donnie was there and had to explain why he was chasing me. And we both got in trouble, but he got it worse than me, because he was older than me, so he knew better. We both had to apologize. During the holidays between Christmas and New Year's, Mom and Dad had gone to a party. Sissy, aka Maxine, was to watch over us, and she did. We were all in bed, and it was late. Sissy and I shared the same room; her bed was by the window and my bed was by the steps up against the wall. The light fixture was over my bed, and for me to reach the light I had to stand up on my bed and grab the long string to pull and turn the light on. Well, when I heard who I thought was Mom and Dad coming up the steps, I leaped up to turn the light on, and it wasn't Mom or Dad; it was a white man. Sissy saw him, and she flew past me and him and ran over to Grandmom Rachael, where our baby brother Sherman was. Our brother came to the house, but the man had gone. But we knew who he was, because he lived in the town and Mom worked with his mother. He was picked up and prosecuted for breaking and entering, and the best thing that came out of this was he didn't get our sister. Thank God.

The night that Mom and Dad went out to party, somehow Mom twisted her ankle and had to have it operated on. She had to have some metal plates inserted into her leg and a cast put on. Well, that was in itself rough, and then we found out that Mom was with child. Oh my, that was even worse. It wasn't bad that she was pregnant, but we knew that there was a chance that she would have to deliver with the cast on. We just wondered how that was to happen. We had to do most things for Mom, which we wanted to do, even though she could get around with a cane. Well, the time came when she went into labor, and we all were there, and we were coaching her. She always was a strong lady, and I do mean strong. She was ready to be taken to the hospital, so Dad took her, and they promised to let us know if and when Mom had the baby. It was a great time for us, knowing that we were going to have another brother or sister. The girls wanted Mom to have a girl, because we had enough boys but just us three girls. Well, the news came, and it was a bouncing baby boy. The girls had lost, and here comes another boy. We all were happy for Mom and for Dad, and we loved having another person in our family. They named him William George, aka Billy. I think he was named after Dad's father. I can remember Dad's brother,

Francis. He was a great uncle and the father of our first cousins, and he also was married to our favorite aunt, Cornelia Brady, aka Aunt Sister, whom we love dearly. Well, I can remember when he passed away. His car had broken down on the road right outside of the city where we lived, and Uncle Francis was pushing the car when he had a heart attack. And from that he passed. God love him, because we did. At the age I was, I can remember him, because Dad and Uncle Francis, aka Putsey and Dad, were very much alike, and they looked alike too. He was a great father also. We miss and love you, Uncle Putsey. Back when our uncle Woodley was living, he used to dance with us, and he danced with his cane. We were always playing music, and he enjoyed us very much, so we started dancing like him, with the stiff leg and cane, and we named the dance the "Uncle Woodley." It caught everyone's eye, and soon it became *the* dance that we all were doing. If he only knew just how popular his dance was; thank you Uncle Woodley. We had fun with that. Our dad was also a really good singer. He liked country, and sometimes when Dad was feeling good, he would come home and start singing and serenading under Mom's bedroom window. That would make her so mad, but he was just showing her love, and he would sing the song "Your Cheatin' Heart." I think Mom didn't want everyone to hear him. I would just laugh, and Mom would tell us to go and get him to come in; he was always doing that. It was funny. He was a funny dad, and there were many times that he would send me to the store to get his ice cream; he loved butter almond. Now mind you, Dad had nooooo teeth, and it tickled me to see how he was going to manage this. But what he would do was cut a cantaloupe in half and seed it and then put the ice cream in the hole of the cantaloupe; he would eat the ice cream, suck on the nuts, and take them out of his mouth. I said, "Dad, why don't you just get vanilla or an ice cream that you can eat?" And he said that he liked the taste. It was just a waste, but he would always get it, and that would bag us all up. It seemed to us to be a waste, but that is what he wanted. The following week we were going on a church picnic, and our dad was taking a nap. Mom wanted us to go and get the tickets, so she sent us upstairs to get the money to purchase them from Dad. Well, we did go up there to wake Dad up, and we couldn't wake him, so we went back downstairs to tell Mom that we could not wake Dad. She then went upstairs to get him up, and I can remember that Mom started crying and told one of us to call 911 because she could not wake him either. So she sent all of us out of the house, and we all wanted to know what was going on and whether we should call the paramedics. We knew that something was going on with Dad. What we didn't know was that he had passed away in his sleep from a heart attack. There was nothing the paramedics could do. Now before all this happened, our baby brother was having a birthday coming in a week, and Dad had gotten him a watch, and he was so excited. And he knew that Billy would be excited too. So he wanted to give him his gift before the day of his birthday. Well, Mom told Dad no, and to just wait, but Dad insisted. So Mom gave in and told him that if he wanted to he could go ahead and give it to him. "If it makes you happy just give it to him." So he did, and Billy was so happy to get his first watch; he really thought he was something then. It made him think he was grown then, because big men wore watches. Well, we think that Dad had a premonition that he would not be here for Billy's birthday, and that is why he was so anxious to give him his birthday gift. After all that happened, we all were glad that he did. It seemed that time had stopped and that it was the end of our lives. Mom tried to comfort all of us, but we knew that we had to comfort her, which we all did. Dad's sister, our aunt Thelma, held Dad's viewing at her home. At that time back in the days that is what we did. We didn't have our viewings at the funeral homes; we did at our own homes. When they were bringing the body into Aunt Thelma's house they could not get the casket through the doors, so they tried to bring it through the window, and they had to turn the casket on its side. This moved his body around, and somehow that messed with his appearance. I cannot remember viewing his body, because they had to take him back to redo what had been disturbed, which was the fluids in his body. That was one of the worst days in our lives. After it was all over, we still got to go to the church picnic. But it was not the same, and although we all tried to enjoy ourselves, we were missing a very big part of our puzzle.

After all that took place, we all thought Mom would be lonely, and we didn't know how we would feel if Mom start dating another man. We were selfish, because we didn't want that. We just wanted to keep her to ourselves. No man could come between Mom and us after our dad. But we knew that she needed someone too, and after about five years, Mom met a man and they became friends. Well, he had to really grow on us before we accepted him, even though we knew he was good for her and she needed that. So if it made her happy, who were we to interfere? He was the second-best thing in her life. To us he then became Mom's friend. But we all had our guard up for protecting our mom, and we all did that. But he was a nice man. When our baby sister had her son, Mr. Eddie, which is what we all called him, was a real grandfather to him. He bought little Skip everything and was very protective of him. In return Skip also loved Mr. Eddie. Skip would always travel with Mom and me wherever we went. If he wasn't with us, he was with Mr. Eddie. I kept him with me most of the time so Mom and Mr. Eddie didn't have to keep him. Skip would always cry to go with me, so away he went with me. My daughter Dawn would also love to have him with her. She did many things for him and with him. He was in love with cowboy boots, and many times he would go to sleep with them on his feet. But don't try to take them off of him; the minute you touched his feet, oh lord he would wake up and you would not get the cowboy boots off. He slept in them. He is a great nephew and now has five children—four boys that are the spitting image of him and one daughter who is spoiled by him and his grandmother. The boys are spoiled by their grandfather, and they just love being spoiled rotten. They are all a joy, and they all have names that start with A, because their dad's name is Ashien. His oldest son is named after him, Ashien Jr.; and then there is his daughter, Azuana. The only child who is not named with an A is De'Naaz. And that is his family. At most holiday times, or when we were getting ready for school, Mom would take us to get new clothes and new shoes and anything else that we needed. All of us would get our clothes and shoes, except our brother, Gaylord, aka Skippy. Mom always had a time finding shoes for Skippy, because he had wide and short feet, so that made it hard to find him shoes. Mom found a store that carried his size, but we were mad because we all had ours and had to go here and there for him, so he inherited the name "Flintstone Feet." When it was time for the boys to go for haircuts, most of the time I would go with them. We walked from our house to a little town that sat alone but still in our town. It was separated from town by a little bridge, and it was called Pokie Town. I used to hate walking across that bridge, so I used to run across. And they would laugh and call me scaredy-cat. I didn't care what I was called. I think I was scared of bridges, because it seemed that I would have dreams about bridges every night. And in my dream I was pulling myself out of the water by a rope, as in Tarzan, and I am still that way. Well, we got to Mr. Celler's house where his barber shop was on his porch. While the boys were getting their hair cut, I played with his granddaughter until they were done. Down from Mr. Celler was another juke joint, called Mr. Harry's; it was a bar and a dance place. It was a place for all of us where we went to enjoy ourselves. It was called Boot, and because everyone in it was our aunts and uncles we called it Uncle Boot, where we danced. Bands would come in and play music, and we had so much fun; the music was great. Another place we would go to enjoy the dance and music would be in another town, called Middle, where the dances were held at the school called Redd. We had to catch a bus to get there, and we did. When I didn't have money to go, and Mom and Dad didn't, I just went to my aunt Thelma, and she would give me what I needed to go. We all danced until the night was over. Those were the days. We did a lot of roller skating. We would all meet at the fire hall, which was right at the next block from our house, and we would skate all around town. We would do tricks and all kind of formations. Most of the time we would have an audience watching us, and that made us feel like we were doing something, but we were good.

Back to our mom: She was the kind of person who owned her own cars but would seldom drive them, but I think she had them just for her children. Whenever she needed to go anywhere, I was usually the one to take her. She would always want me to take her, so I became driving Mrs. Brady, not driving Miss Daisy. Where she went, I went; we were like sisters, friends, and companions, and most of all she was my Mom. She was my all and all. Some of the things that Mom would do just bagged me up. She was a very outspoken person, but only when she needed to be. For instance, once we were together and Mom was hungry, so she ordered a hot dog from a man. Well, the man was fixing it and Mom happened to see him scratch his butt. Oh my God! Well, she let him finish fixing it, and then I wondered if she saw what he did, and when he handed it to her, she said, "Now, do you really think that I am going to eat that hot dog?"
He responded, "Did you order a hot dog?"
She said, ". . . after you had just scratched your butt." Well, she told him to eat it, because she was not going to. And we left with him still holding the hot dog. And you know what I did? Well, I just bagged up. Because you should have seen the look on his face; it was sooooo funny. But she was right. We know that people that are serving you food do those things. But we don't see it, and

we don't know unless we see it. And we would do the very same thing that our mom did. Great job, Mom; kudos. That was one thing that we loved about our mom—she was a very very strong lady and very honest and respected by all. She tried to instill the same values in her children. Three of her children were in the military at some point. Well, when they came home, there was a big army trunk that had their clothes and whatever else was in it. I think it was Doggie's, but I think Skippy used it for some stuff he had. Well, on this day Mom was cleaning, and she went into the trunk to clean it out, and she discovered some kind of stuff that didn't look right to her. So she started investigating: She had all of us line up, and then she showed us the stuff she found, and she asked all of us who it belonged to. Well, Sissy didn't know, and I didn't know even what it was. Shelly was a baby, so she didn't know, which meant that all of us girls were excused. So the boys were left to answer her questions, but none of them claimed to know anything about it. So she took all the boys to the bathroom, and, me being me, I followed, and then she took the stuff and poured it into the toilet and flushed it down. She said it don't belong to anyone now. Well, I still didn't know what it was and who it belonged to, but we soon found out who it belonged to. The culprit was Skippy, and it hurt him so much to see it flushed. Hahahaha. That is what you got for making us all guilty of something you knew you had. Good job, Mom. Kudos to you.

We all got so excited when Mom and Dad said we were getting a color TV—that was when they first came out. One day Dad came home with a plastic screen, and we all wondered what it was. Well, it was our color TV. The color screen attached to the front of our black and white to make it a color TV. We were happy just to see how it would work. We were looking at blue and green and yellow and red people and green skies and green rivers, but we had color. That was soooo funny, but later we did get a real color TV. And that was great.

Since I was the tomboy, I used to play with most of the boys, and they would come to get me to play baseball in the field across from our home. One day we were playing, and I hit the ball and was running to the base, and I had to slide. The boy who was playing the base saw that I was bleeding and told me that I had cut myself. I looked down and saw the blood, and I flew home to tell Mom that I cut myself by sliding into the base. Well, she looked at it and started laughing. Then I was wondering what Mom was laughing at—did she not hear what I said, that I was cut somewhere? Then she said to me that I was not cut. I had started my monthly, and I wondered what she meant. Duh, then she had to explain that to me. Well, we didn't know about the birds and the bees, because our family didn't talk about it, not until they had to. And that was the time Mom had to talk to me. But I felt so bad—now how do I tell my friends that I really didn't cut myself, but that it was a female thing? Well, I had to tell them that it wasn't a bad cut, and that Mom had to put some peroxide on it. I told a little white lie. Hahaha. Oh well—they will never know. After dinner, or supper, as we called it, I would take my brother Skippy and sister Shelly up to our school so they could play on the swings and the sliding board. Skippy was about five or six, and Shelly was three or four; they both enjoyed that. Well, you know that every town has a town bully, and we did. It was a girl named Wenny. She was bothering the other kids, stopping them from swinging and stopping them from sliding down the sliding board. Shelly and Skippy were having a good time, and then the bully started with them, and I told her to leave them alone. She didn't; she just kept on bothering them. So, me being me, I had a fight with her, and I got the best of her. And then I took Shelly and Skippy home. She didn't think I could beat her, but she found out that I could. And guess what? I didn't have any more problems from her, because she had met her match. The moral of the story is, don't be a bully because you never know when you will meet your match.

At every Christmas at our house, we always knew two things that would be under the Christmas tree when we got it: a pool table and an electric football game for Billy. The pool table was great, because we all could shoot pool. But that football game was a joke. It was a vibrating football field, and you would put little men on it, and they just vibrated across the field. They went in all kinds of directions, and I have yet to see the man holding the football cross over the goal line for a touchdown. It was a crazy game. We would always get our Christmas tree the day before Christmas, so we didn't enjoy the days leading up to Christmas. But when we did get it, it was like yea, finally we knew what was next. And that was our goodies—our toys, clothes, and shoes. We were so excited to get our new things. In our little town, we didn't have too many exciting things that went on, except that we did have the greatest fireworks around; we had people come from all around to see them. Our town would be overrun with cars, so many that you couldn't find a parking space and you had to walk for a couple of miles to get to the end of town where the fireworks were held. We would have all kinds of vendors selling a little bit of everything from food to souvenirs. And there would be boat rides all day long to Pea Patch Island. It was a very good day for our city; we had the best fireworks around. We had big barbeques at our family's house. We played games, pitched horseshoes, and played some card games. It was so much fun, spending a day in our historic town.

THE END AS I KNOW IT.
I also dedicate this book to the rest of our family,

Brother Gaylord, aka Skippy Brady
Brother William, aka Billy Brady

and to my sisters

Sister Maxine, aka Sissy Brady Young
Sister Rachell, aka Shelly Brady

and this book is dedicated to my husband, Harold Moore

and to my two children, Dawn and Harold Moore Jr.

and to our special aunt, Cornelia Brady,
whom we love dearly

and to me
Patricia Brady Moore, aka Patsy Brady Moore

written by Patricia Brady Moore

www.ingramcontent.com/pod-product-compliance
Lightning Source LLC
Chambersburg PA
CBHW061225280526
45784CB00006B/2629